AUSTRALIA'S MOST
ADVENTUROUS

—

By Karen McGhee

Australian GEOGRAPHIC

AUSTRALIA'S MOST
ADVENTUROUS

Australia's Most Adventurous is published by Australian Geographic, an imprint of Bauer Media Ltd. All images and text are copyright © Bauer Media and may not be reproduced without the written permission of the publishers.

First published in 2015 by:

MEDIA GROUP

Bauer Media
54 Park Street, Sydney, NSW 2000
Telephone: (02) 9263 9813
Fax: (02) 9216 3731
Email: editorial@ausgeo.com.au

www.australiangeographic.com.au

Australian Geographic customer service:
1300 555 176 (local call rate within Australia).
From overseas +61 2 8667 5295

Printed in China by Leo Paper Products Ltd.

Funds from the sale of this book go to support the Australian Geographic Society, a not-for-profit organisation dedicated to sponsoring conservation and scientific projects, as well as adventures and expeditions.

Editor Lauren Smith
Text Karen McGhee
Book design Katharine McKinnon
Picture research Maisie Keep & Jess Teideman
Print production Chris Clear
Sub-editor Amy Russell
Proofreader Ken Eastwood
Managing director David Goodchild
Publishing director – Specialist Division Cornelia Schulze
Publisher Jo Runciman
Editor-in-chief, Australian Geographic Chrissie Goldrick

RELATED TITLES:

The Australian Geographic Society awards conservationists and adventurers every year. Look for this medallion to meet our past winners!

AUSTRALIA'S MOST ADVENTUROUS

Throughout Australia's history, many men and women have sought to reach new heights, break records and see the planet from a new perspective.

CONTENTS

SUMMIT SCALERS

These adventurers made it all the way to the top!

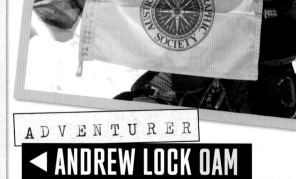

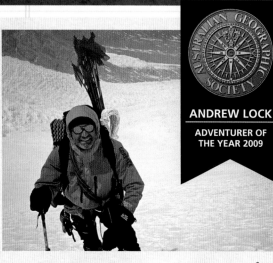

ANDREW LOCK

ADVENTURER OF THE YEAR 2009

To the limit!

In 2012 Andrew was near the top on his second climb of Mount Everest and developed symptoms of cerebral oedema, which is caused by high-altitude conditions. His symptoms included vomiting and blurred vision. Andrew felt the darkness was rushing at him, he says, and he knew it was time to quit climbing big mountains!

ADVENTURER
◄ ANDREW LOCK OAM

There are 14 mountains in the world higher than 8000m and Andrew Lock was the first Australian (and only, so far) to reach the top of all of them. He was only the 18th person in the world to achieve this amazing feat. It took Andrew 16 years, starting with Pakistan's K2 – the second-highest mountain, after Everest. Tragically, while climbing down from K2, two members of Andrew's expedition team fell to their deaths. Andrew came very close to losing his own life on the last climb, on Tibet's Mount Shishapangma in 2009. He and his climbing partner were forced to spend a harrowing night on a narrow ledge just below the summit without a tent and in temperatures of –30°C.

LINCOLN HALL
LIFETIME OF
ADVENTURE 2010

CLIMBER

▶ LINCOLN HALL OAM

This renowned mountaineer climbed more than 40 of the world's toughest mountains in seven countries. He was the chief organiser of the first Australian expedition to climb Mount Everest, in 1984, but on that historic occasion wasn't part of the group that reached the summit. Lincoln finally scaled Everest in 2006, but collapsed in the mountain's so-called Death Zone as he began climbing down. His team was forced to leave him for dead a few hundred metres below the summit. The next day he was found clinging to life and lived to tell the tale after being rescued.

Did you know?

Despite risking his life on mountains the world over, it wasn't climbing that led to Lincoln's early death in 2012 at the age 56, but the disease mesothelioma. It was found to have been caused by his exposure to **asbestos** while building a cubby house with his dad when he was young.

SUE FEAR

SPIRIT OF ADVENTURE 1999

ADVENTURER OF THE YEAR 2003

LIFETIME OF ADVENTURE 2006

Did you know?

Everest mountaineers, Sue Fear, Edmund Hillary and George Mallory all tackled the peak with their era's best clothing and equipment.

CLIMBER
◄ SUE FEAR OAM

Sue was one of Australia's greatest female mountain climbers. In 2003 she became the second Australian woman to reach the top of Mount Everest. She was also the first Australian woman to climb Everest by using the North Ridge Route, which is technically harder than the Southern Route used by most people to reach the top of this massive mountain. Tragically, in 2006, at the age of just 43, Sue fell into a crevasse as she was climbing down from the summit of Nepal's Mount Manaslu, the world's eighth-highest mountain. Her body was never found.

CLIMBER
► BRIGITTE MUIR OAM

In 1997 Brigitte became the first Australian woman to reach the top of Everest: it was her fourth attempt to climb the huge mountain. She was also the first Australian to climb the 'Seven Summits' – the highest mountain on each continent. Brigitte was born in Belgium, and began dreaming of adventure when she was a child. She came to live in Australia in 1983 and became an Australian citizen in 1987.

Muir motivation

Brigitte's life was changed when she heard the phrase "We must live our dreams, not dream our lives." It's been her motto ever since.

BRIGITTE MUIR

SPIRIT OF ADVENTURE 1997

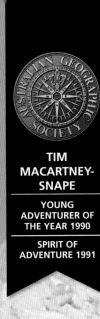
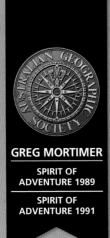

TIM MACARTNEY-SNAPE

YOUNG ADVENTURER OF THE YEAR 1990

SPIRIT OF ADVENTURE 1991

GREG MORTIMER

SPIRIT OF ADVENTURE 1989

SPIRIT OF ADVENTURE 1991

Did you know?

In 1990 Tim became the first person in the world to walk from sea level to the top of Mount Everest.

SUMMIT SCALERS

CLIMBERS

▶ TIM MACARTNEY-SNAPE OAM & GREG MORTIMER OAM

On October 3 1984, Tim Macartney-Snape and Greg Mortimer became the first Australians to reach the top of Mount Everest. They were also the first people in the world to reach the top by climbing its north face – and they did it without carrying oxygen tanks! Both Tim and Greg also achieved many other mountain-climbing firsts. In 1990, for example, Greg became the first Australian to climb Pakistan's K2, the world's second-highest mountain. Also that year he became the first Australian to climb the highest mountain in Antarctica, Vinson Massif.

WATER
WONDERS

Diving deep or going the distance, these heroes have spent years in the water!

Did you know?

In 2008 Ron and Valerie Taylor won an Australian Geographic Society's Lifetime of Conservation Award for 50 years of underwater conservation work, including groundbreaking research into shark behaviour.

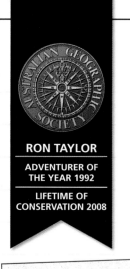

RON TAYLOR

ADVENTURER OF
THE YEAR 1992

LIFETIME OF
CONSERVATION 2008

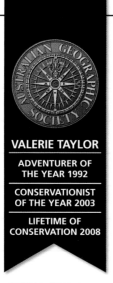

VALERIE TAYLOR

ADVENTURER OF
THE YEAR 1992

CONSERVATIONIST
OF THE YEAR 2003

LIFETIME OF
CONSERVATION 2008

DIVERS

▶ RON AND VALERIE TAYLOR OAM

Ron and Valerie Taylor were two of the world's first marine **conservationists**. Ron's interest in the ocean began with spearfishing during the 1950s. He was also a keen photographer and soon became more interested in shooting underwater life with a camera than with a spear. From the 1960s onwards, Ron and Valerie became outspoken advocates for the protection of ocean environments and the creatures living in them...particularly big sharks!

WATER WONDERS

Did you know?

Ron and Valerie Taylor were the first people to film sharks at night. They proved it was a myth that sharks need to constantly keep moving and were also the first people to film great white sharks under water, with and without a cage!

Did you know?

"I guess it's a bit wacky to live under water in a box made of recycled steel with plants as a life support," Lloyd admitted after his experiment. "But having achieved that has been so rewarding."

INVENTOR

◀ LLOYD GODSON

Marine biologist Lloyd Godson says he has ''wild ideas" that he likes to put to the test. In 2007 he attracted worldwide media attention when he lived in a steel chamber 3m under water in a wetland, in the NSW city of Albury, for 12 days without assistance. The project was funded by the Australian Geographic Society and was really a huge experiment devised by Lloyd to see if he could survive using the type of self-contained life-support system that could one day make long-distance space travel possible. He used algae to recycle part of his waste and produce some of the oxygen he breathed, and he made his own electricity by pedalling a bicycle. To the left, you can see what the inside of his biosub looked like.

Record breaker

Lloyd Godson holds the Guinness World Record for the 'most electricity generated by pedalling under water' and is now an ambassador for ocean exploration.

ANDREW HUGHES
SPIRIT OF ADVENTURE 2009

ECO - WARRIOR
◄ ANDREW HUGHES

This Tasmanian teacher doesn't use the usual sort of classroom for his lessons. Instead, in a project he now calls Expedition Class, he teaches both primary and high school students from wilderness locations. His lessons are conducted via satellite and his subjects include conservation, the natural world, survival and adventure. Andrew began his life as an 'adventure teacher' in 2006, when he paddled 5000km from Hobart to Cape York in a kayak through rough seas infested with sharks and crocodiles.

SWIMMER
▼ SUSIE MARONEY

In 1997, aged 22, Susie Maroney became the first person to swim from Cuba to the United States. It was an epic 180km feat that took just over 24 hours of non-stop swimming – inside a wire cage to keep her safe from sharks, and smothered in petroleum jelly for protection from jellyfish stings! Susie's body was pounded by 3–4m waves: she became seasick and hallucinated about monkeys.

Hard worker

What makes Susie Maroney's feats particularly remarkable is that she was born with cerebral palsy – a life-long physical disability that limits the body's movements.

TAMMY VAN WISSE
ADVENTURER OF THE YEAR 2001

SUSIE MARONEY
SPIRIT OF ADVENTURE 1997

SWIMMER
▲ TAMMY VAN WISSE

During two decades as a marathon swimmer, Tammy Van Wisse swam more than 65,000km – equivalent to swimming 1.5 times around the world. One of her greatest feats was swimming the length of the Murray River – Australia's longest river. Tammy began her swim in November 2000 and it took her 160 days to cover a distance of 2438km; so far she's the only person to have done it.

PILOT PIONEERS

These high flyers chased their dreams up into the clouds.

PILOT

▼ TERRY MCCORMACK

Terry McCormack piloted Australia's first modern hot-air balloon on 4 July 1964. It took place in a paddock, in the western NSW town of Parkes and was the first manned balloon flight in Australia in almost 50 years. It lasted 30 minutes, took Terry 5km away and was watched by thousands of onlookers.

Did you know?

As a boy, Bert Hinkler studied the flight of ibises, which are wading birds, and strapped wings on his back in an attempt to fly.

PILOT

▲ BERT HINKLER

In 1928 pioneering **aviator** and inventor Bert Hinkler became the first person to fly solo from England to Australia. It was a feat he achieved in a record-breaking 15 days. He was also the first person to fly solo across the South Atlantic Ocean, in 1931. Bert was killed in 1933 at the age of 40 when his plane crashed into a mountain range in Italy during another attempt at a record-breaking flight.

PILOT

◄ LINDA CORBOULD OAM

When, in 1981, Linda Corbould first joined the Royal Australian Air Force (RAAF), she wasn't able to fly for the RAAF because she was a woman. Women were eventually allowed to train as pilots from 1990 onwards and Linda was the third to complete her flight training. In 2006 she became the first woman to command an RAAF flying **squadron**. Linda was also a champion skydiver. She represented Australia in the sport's 1985 world championships, in Turkey.

PILOT

▲ MAUDE BONNEY OAM

Australian pilot Maude 'Lores' Bonney set and broke many records during her career as a pioneering aviatrix. In 1931 she made the longest one-day flight by a woman (1600km). She was also the first woman to **circumnavigate** Australia by air, in 1932, and fly solo from Australia to England, in 1933. In 1937 she became the first person to fly from Australia to South Africa.

Danger above

During the early days of flight, many pioneering aviators lost their lives when they were young because it was such a new and dangerous pursuit. Two notable exceptions were Maude Bonney, who died at the age of 96 in 1994, and Nancy-Bird Walton, who died aged 93 in 2009.

PILOT

◄ NANCY-BIRD WALTON AO

As she was born with the surname Bird, it isn't surprising that Nancy took to the skies! In 1934, at the age of just 19, she became the youngest licensed female pilot in the British Commonwealth. During the next five years Nancy went on to work as a pilot for the Far West Children's Health Scheme – flying doctors, nurses and sick patients on life-saving missions to some of the most remote parts of NSW. She was celebrated as the 'Angel of the Outback' and became known as Nancy-Bird Walton when she married Charles Walton in 1939. Her exploits as a pilot made her so famous during the 1930s that she was invited to dine with kings, queens and Hollywood stars.

Did you know?

Smithy became famous as the 'world's greatest pilot' before disappearing in 1935 without a trace while flying off the coast of Burma, in South-East Asia.

PILOT

▲ CHARLES KINGSFORD SMITH

Not long after aviation began, Brisbane-born Charles Kingsford Smith learned to fly during World War I. 'Smithy', as he was known, went on to pioneer Australia's commercial aviation industry. But he was also a great adventurer and set many world flight records – at a time when planes were made from wood, wire, fabric and not much else.

Number one

Charles Kingsford Smith made the first flight across the Pacific Ocean from the USA to Australia, and the first non-stop flight across the Australian mainland, both in 1928. Smithy was knighted in 1932 for his services to aviation and has featured on Australia's $20 note.

SPACE EXPLORERS

Some adventures will take you out of this world.

ASTRONAUT

▶ ANDY THOMAS AO

No other Australian has spent as much time in space as Adelaide-born engineer and **NASA** astronaut Andy Thomas. His first flight into space was in May 1996 on board the space shuttle *Endeavour*. His fourth and final mission above the Earth was in 2005 on the space shuttle *Discovery*. All up, Andy spent a total of 177 days in space during four flights.

Out of this world!

In 1998 Andy spent 141 days in space on board the space shuttle *Discovery* and then the space station Mir. He completed 2250 orbits of planet Earth during that time.

ASTRONAUT
▲ PAUL SCULLY-POWER AM

Oceanographer Paul Scully-Power was the first Australian-born person in space. Paul worked as a senior scientist and scuba diver with both the US and Australian navies and developed a high level of expertise in the oceans and the physical forces that drive them. In October 1984, he flew as a scientist on the space shuttle *Challenger* during an 8-day NASA study of Earth sciences. By the time he landed back on Earth, Paul had travelled more than 5.4 million kilometres, orbited our planet 133 times and spent more than 197 hours in space.

ASTRONAUT
◄ PHILIP CHAPMAN

Philip Chapman was the first Australian-born astronaut. In 1967 he became the first person born outside of America to be selected as a NASA astronaut and was involved in preparations for several moon missions. Philip never made it into space but logged more than 1000 hours of flying time in jet aircraft.

After graduating from Sydney University with a physics degree, Philip spent 15 months in 1957–58 in Antarctica studying the phenomenon known as aurora australis. After spending the polar winter during that time living in a packing crate at a remote two-man camp, he was awarded the British Polar Medal.

DOUBLE TROUBLE

Sometimes you need a buddy to get where you want to go!

CHRIS BRAY

YOUNG ADVENTURER OF THE YEAR 2004

SPIRIT OF ADVENTURE 2008

CLARK CARTER

SPIRIT OF ADVENTURE 2008

ADVENTURERS
▲ CLARK CARTER AND CHRIS BRAY

It took these two adventurers and filmmakers four years of planning and two attempts to complete a world-first crossing – on foot and unsupported – of Victoria Island, in the Arctic. This is the world's eighth largest island, and most of it is unexplored and uninhabited. Clark and Chris first braved blizzards, mud-pits and polar bears in 2005 to attempt the 1100km crossing. But they were forced to give up after making it less than one-third of the way. They buried the Australian Geographic Society flag and vowed to return for it one day and finish their journey. They did this in 2009, completing the last 700km of the crossing in a gruelling 128 days.

A hard trek!

"Victoria Island threw up every conceivable obstacle – from hail, twister clouds and bucketing rain, to intimidating musk-ox bulls and fields of metre-deep moss, mazes of canyon-like valleys and jumbled patches," Chris Bray wrote in his account of his and Clark's epic crossing of Victoria Island.

DON MCINTYRE

SPIRIT OF
ADVENTURE 1993

ADVENTURER OF
THE YEAR 1996

LIFETIME OF
ADVENTURE 2012

MARGIE MCINTYRE

ADVENTURER OF
THE YEAR 1996

ADVENTURERS

▲ DON & MARGIE MCINTYRE

This husband-and-wife adventure team shared the 1996 Australian Geographic Society (AGS) Adventurer of the Year Award in 1996 after they spent 1995 living in a box, chained to rocks at the windiest place on Earth – the site of Mawson's Huts, in Antarctica. And when Don received the AGS Lifetime of Adventure award in 2012, he agreed he couldn't have done it without his former partner Margie. She's been involved in some way with all of Don's extraordinary adventures for the past three decades, joining him when she could or helping to plan and make them happen.

Helping Hands

In 2007 Margie provided the crucial support Don needed to complete a world-first solo ultra-light gyrocopter flight around Australia – 13,000km in 22 days. And in 2010, with Margie's help, Don and three others sailors travelled 7408km in a 7.5m open boat across the Pacific Ocean, retracing the legendary 1789 voyage of Captain William Bligh. Bligh and a few supporters were set afloat on a small boat after his crew mutinied and took command of his ship the *Bounty*.

JAMES 'CAS' CASTRISSION & JUSTIN 'JONESY' JONES

YOUNG
ADVENTURER OF
THE YEAR 2008

SPIRIT OF
ADVENTURE 2012

ADVENTURERS

▲ JAMES 'CAS' CASTRISSION & JUSTIN 'JONESY' JONES

If you think all the great Australian explorers are historical figures, then meet Cas and Jonesy! They met at high school in Sydney in the 1990s and have been discovering the world around them in a series of adventurous expeditions since 2001. They were the first to kayak from Australia to New Zealand without support, and the full length of the Murray River. They were also the first to travel unsupported from the edge of Antarctica to the South Pole unsupported. They plan to keep on with their world-first feats well into the 21st century.

YOUNG ADVENTURERS

Never let age stop you from having a great adventure.

▶ JESSE MARTIN OAM

In 1999 at the age of 18, Jesse became the youngest person to sail around the world – solo, unassisted and non-stop. His boat was called *Lionheart*.

Jesse Martin's solo circumnavigation of the world inspired Jessica Watson to make the same trip.

The big picture!

"I look at the trip as made up of a heap of little things," says Jesse. "If you look at it in the entirety, it's big. But day-to-day, life's just made up of little things."

JESSICA WATSON

YOUNG ADVENTURER OF THE YEAR 2010

SAILOR

◀ JESSICA WATSON OAM

On 15 May 2011, Queenslander Jessica Watson sailed into Sydney Harbour to a celebration almost as big as New Year's Eve. She had been alone at sea for 210 days and, aged just 16, she had just become the youngest person to sail solo and unassisted around the world. Her brave adventure captured the nation's heart and she was welcomed home like a hero by thousands of people in and around Sydney Harbour.

Did you know?

During her 7-month journey of more than 20,0000km around the world on her yacht *Ella's Pink Lady*, Jessica faced storms, loneliness, 12m seas and 140km/h winds.

RYAN CAMPBELL

YOUNG ADVENTURER OF THE YEAR 2013

PILOT

◀ RYAN CAMPBELL

When Ryan Campbell touched down at a small airport south of Sydney on 7 September 2013 he became the youngest person to fly a single-engine aircraft solo around the world. He was also the first teenager to achieve this extraordinary feat that was sponsored by the Australian Geographic Society. It took him 70 days to fly 44,448km in a tiny plane called the *Spirit of the Sapphire Coast*. He was just 19 years old.

Proud parents

"He's always been really focused and committed in whatever he put his mind to, which is why – I think – he's had so much success," Ryan's mum Joanne said after her son's amazing achievement.

ENVIRO CLUB

A connection with the natural world is where great adventures begin.

Did you know?

Dick founded Dick Smith Electronics, the *Australian Geographic* journal and Dick Smith Foods.

DICK SMITH

LIFETIME OF ADVENTURE 2000

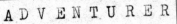

ADVENTURER
▶ DICK SMITH AC

On 18 June 1993 Dick Smith floated into the history books by making the first non-stop flight across Australia in a hot-air balloon. Dick's life of adventure and business success began after he first attempted to climb the world's tallest sea stack, Balls Pyramid, in 1964. Dick's adventures have also included a solo flight around the world in a helicopter (1982–83) and a solo helicopter flight to the North Pole (1987). His passion for the planet led to setting the record for the fastest trip from Perth to Sydney in a solar-powered car in 1994, covering 4200km in 8.5 days.

To the very top!

Balls Pyramid is a rock spire that rises 561m straight up out of the ocean off Lord Howe Island, about 700km north-east of Sydney. Climbing it is exceptionally tough and taught Dick Smith to never give up, no matter how tough a challenge becomes.

ENVIRO CLUB

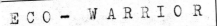

E C O - W A R R I O R

▲ TIM JARVIS AM

Environmental scientist and author Tim Jarvis uses his drive for adventure to highlight the beauty of Earth's natural environments and the problems they face. He was named the Australian Geographic Society's 2013 Adventurer of the Year after he re-enacted the 1916 Antarctic journey by polar explorer Ernest Shackleton. It followed one of the greatest recorded stories of human determination and survival. Tim used the equipment, methods and type of protective clothing available to Shackleton. Previously, Tim had made unsupported expeditions to the South Pole and across Australia's Great Victoria Desert.

Purposed pursuit

Tim holds records for the fastest unsupported journey to the South Pole and longest unsupported journey in Antarctica. His adventuring is bringing the world's attention to the plight of the last equatorial glaciers, which survive at high altitudes on mountains around the equator. These are rapidly disappearing due to climate change.

E C O - W A R R I O R

▲ JEFFREY LEE AM

Jeffrey Lee's adventure has been a cultural one that stretches back thousands of years in time. As the last surviving member of the Djok clan, Jeffrey has a deep connection to the Northern Territory homelands of his people. He's the senior custodian of the 1228ha Kongarra region, which is believed to contain a **uranium** deposit worth many millions of dollars. It could have made Jeffrey one of Australia's richest men. But instead he's made sure that future generations of Australians will get to experience the adventure and beauty of this valuable parcel of land, by ensuring that it's been included as part of the Kakadu World Heritage Area.

GO THE DISTANCE

Epic journeys through amazing environments.

PAT FARMER

ADVENTURER OF THE YEAR 2012

Did you know?

Pat Farmer's record-breaking run across the Earth raised $100,000 for Red Cross clean water and disaster relief projects.

RUNNER

▲ PAT FARMER

Ultra-marathon runner Pat Farmer completed the world's longest run in January 2012. It was an epic journey on foot from the North to the South Pole that's already known as one of the greatest feats of endurance by an Australian. Pat's run across the planet began in April 2011 when he left the North Pole and started pounding a path southwards. From the Arctic he travelled through north, central and south America, and then finally on to Antarctica. He covered an average of 80km a day – about two marathons – and he ran a total distance of 21,000 km.

The extra mile

Pat also completed a record-breaking run around Australia in 1999. He covered 15,000km in 195 days, going through 14 pairs of running shoes in the process.

▲ JON MUIR

Jon Muir is an Australian adventurer, explorer and wanderer. In 2001 he completed the first unassisted crossing of Australia on foot – a feat that has yet to be repeated. He started in tidal salt water near the coastal city of Port Augusta, SA and travelled across mostly desert and savannah grasslands. After 127 days and 2500km, surviving mostly on bush tucker, he reached Burketown, an isolated town on Queensland's Gulf of Carpentaria. Jon has also reached the summit of Mount Everest alone and walked to both the South and North poles.

JON MUIR
ADVENTURER OF
THE YEAR 2002

GO THE DISTANCE

Did you know?

Jon Muir has said that his reason for living is simply to witness nature.

TECH TEAM

Technology brings the best out in some people.

FLYERS

▶ HEATHER SWAN & GLENN SINGLEMAN

This Sydney-based husband and wife team have been notching up world records for almost a decade now. They use high-tech alternatives to parachutes known as wingsuits, which allow them the freedom to manoeuvre through the air at high altitudes as if they are flying. They flew across Sydney Harbour in 2011, and in January 2015 they were part of a team that made the first wingsuit crossing over Brisbane. Also in 2015, they were part of the first team to make a wingsuit flight across the Grand Canyon in the USA.

HEATHER SWAN

SPIRIT OF ADVENTURE 2006

GLENN SINGLEMAN

SPIRIT OF ADVENTURE 1994

SPIRIT OF ADVENTURE 2006

Take the leap!

Glenn and Heather are also known for their feats in **BASE-jumping**, which is parachuting from a fixed structure rather than a plane. They hold the record for the world's highest BASE-jump in a wingsuit – 6672m from Mount Meru in the Indian Himalayas.

ADVENTURER

▲ RON ALLUM

This former ABC radio engineer is a legend of the deep...literally. His inventiveness and technical knowhow made it possible for Canadian adventurer and movie director James Cameron to mount a record-breaking expedition to one of Earth's last frontiers – the deepest known part of the ocean. Ron was the co-designer and pilot of the highly specialised submersible used by James in 2012 to reach the location known as Challenger Deep. It's at the bottom of the world's deepest ocean trench – the Marianas Trench – in the Pacific Ocean; 11km below the ocean's surface. Thanks largely to Ron, James became the third person to reach Challenger Deep and the first to do so by himself. As well as being famed for his technical skills, Ron is also one of the world's most accomplished cave divers.

Deep down

Challenger Deep is as inaccessible as outer space! It's so deep that if Everest, Earth's tallest mountain, was dropped here it would be covered by more than 2km of water! The pressure exerted by all this water is 1000 times what it is at the surface – one of the major difficulties Ron had to deal with.

A LONG JOURNEY

Sometimes you've just got to get away.

ADVENTURER

▲ TIM COPE

Adventurer and filmmaker Tim Cope grew up in Victoria, but he's spent much of his adult life trekking and travelling. In 1999, at the age of 20, he cycled from Russia to China through the forests of Siberia and deserts of Mongolia. Tim was named the Australian Geographic Society's Adventurer of the Year in 2006, after spending three years travelling 10,000km on horseback, from Mongolia to Hungary.

TIM COPE

SPIRIT OF ADVENTURE 2001

YOUNG ADVENTURER OF THE YEAR 2002

ADVENTURER OF THE YEAR 2006

ADVENTURER
▼ ROBYN DAVIDSON

Robyn Davidson's trek across Australia with four camels and a dog became the subject of a best-selling book called *Tracks* and then a Hollywood movie. When Robyn set out from Alice Springs in 1977 and headed west across the desert to the Indian Ocean, she told only a few people what she was planning. But when an American photographer met her by chance before she left Alice Springs, he decided to document her epic nine-month 2700km journey. That's when her story went international.

KAY COTTEE
SPIRIT OF ADVENTURE 1989

Did you know?

Robyn's story of hardship in the Aussie desert captured the imagination of people around the world...and she's been widely known as the 'camel lady' ever since.

SAILOR
▲ KAY COTTEE AO

Kay Cottee became a role model for girls all over the world when, in 1988, she became the first woman to sail around the world – on her own, without help and non-stop. The trip took her 189 days. Kay was named 1988 Australian of the Year.

Born to do it

Because Kay was born into a yachting family, she was only a few weeks old when she was taken sailing for the first time. "I spent a lot of time gazing out to sea from my classroom window," admits Kay, who didn't like school.

SNOW

Facing the cold and braving the elements.

SCOUTS

AUSTRALIAN GEOGRAPHIC SOCIETY

LINDA BEILHARZ

ADVENTURER OF THE YEAR 2010

SKIER

▶ LINDA BEILHARZ OAM

In 2004 Linda Beilharz became the first Australian woman to ski from the edge of Antarctica to the South Pole, the largest **ice cap** on Earth. She was the first, and so far only, Aussie woman to do it. Linda's ski trip there inspired her to travel across the next three largest ice caps; the Arctic, Greenland and Patagonia. In 2007 she successfully crossed the Greenland ice cap and in 2009 Linda attempted a crossing of South Patagonia. She wasn't successful, but it didn't discourage Linda from setting off to ski across the Arctic. In 2010 she completed an epic 55-day, 780km journey from the most northern tip of Canada to the North Pole. She became the first Australian woman to trek to the North Pole. In 2012, she completed the South Patagonia Icecap crossing, and said she was all the wiser for having tried before.

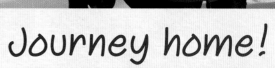

Journey home!

After returning from her Greenland journey, Linda set up a not-for-profit company called Journeys for Learning. She uses stories from her expeditions to teach children about resilience, teamwork and environmental sustainability.

ADVENTURER

▲ SIR DOUGLAS MAWSON

This Australian geologist was one of the most remarkable early Antarctic explorers. He visited the frozen continent repeatedly, at a time when getting there was as difficult and dangerous as getting into space is now. Douglas Mawson was part of a team that, in 1908, first climbed Antarctica's Mount Erebus, the Earth's most southerly active volcano. He led several expeditions to Antarctica, including the 1911–14 Australasian Antarctic Expedition that explored thousands of kilometres of Antarctic coastline and gathered important biological, geological and other scientific information.

Ski science

Of all the early Antarctic explorers, Douglas Mawson is considered to have contributed the most to science. Mawson and his team set up two bases with huts in Antarctica where men could stay and work for weeks on end. One was at Cape Denison – now known as Earth's windiest place – and the main hut there is still standing after more than 100 years.

SYDNEY KIRKBY

ADVENTURER OF
THE YEAR 1997

ADVENTURER

▲ SYDNEY KIRKBY MBE(C)

During the 20 years up to 1980, no-one explored and mapped more unknown parts of the Earth than Australian Antarctic **surveyor** Sydney Kirkby. Between 1956 and 1980, Sydney went to Antarctica five times, during which he lived and travelled across the icy continent for more than five long years. Sydney Kirkby was almost paralysed from the waist down by the disease polio when he was 5 years old. A gruelling rehabilitation program helped restore most of his movement, but he had lasting problems with his right leg and always walked with a limp.

▼ GLOSSARY

Asbestos	A naturally occurring mineral that is used in some building materials and can cause a type of cancer known as mesothelioma.
Aviator	A pilot of an aircraft.
BASE-jumping	BASE stands for building, antenna, span, Earth; BASE-jumping is an extreme sport that involves jumping from these sorts of high fixed structures or cliffs using a parachute or wingsuit .
Conservationist	A person committed to protecting wildlife and the environment.
Circumnavigate	Travel all the way around something, particularly by sea or air.
Ice cap	An extensive area of land that is permanently covered by ice and snow; usually in the Earth's polar regions.
NASA	Stands for National Aeronautics and Space Administration: it's a government agency in the USA that runs one of the world's major space programs.
Oceanographer	A scientist who deals with the features of water in the oceans, including how it moves and the chemicals it contains.
Squadron	A major military unit in an air force; it will contain more than two aircraft.
Surveyor	A person who measures and maps features in a landscape.
Ultra-marathon	An event that involves walking or running a distance that's further than a traditional marathon, which is 42km.
Uranium	A silvery-white metal that can be used as a source of energy.

▼ POST-NOMINALS

Queen Elizabeth established the Order of Australia to recognise the contributions and achievements of the Australian people. There are different awards, and many of the adventurers and risk-takers included in this book have been awarded. This key shows you what the letters after their name (called post-nominals) mean. Sydney Kirkby has also been awarded a civilian Member of the Most Excellent Order of the British Empire (MBE).

AC Companion of the order

AO Officer of the order

AM Member of the order

OAM Medal of the order

PHOTOGRAPHER AND ILLUSTRATOR CREDITS
Page numbers are followed by image position, indicated clockwise from top left of page.